Street Cred:

Rules to the Money Game

Volume I

Khalil Abdul-Aziz

ISBN-13: 978-1500537630
ISBN-10: 1500537632

1. Self-help   2. Academic Publishing – Textbook   3. Handbook – Guides and
manuals

Edited and compiled by Neely Terrell
Book Cover Design & Illustrations by Cameron "Da Illa'strator" Wilson

This book is dedicated to my beautiful mother who worked so hard to instill precious values in me that I reflect on daily. Also my lovely daughters, Khalimah and Shilynn, who I pray for every day. My two brothers, especially the late Codi C, who taught me so much and was my personal mentor. My grandchildren's children's children, please read it, apply it, and pass it on.

Table of Contents

My Story

I hope this book finds you in the best of health and spirit. My prayer is that this book will get you one step closer to financial freedom for yourself as well as your family and community. I wrote this book so you wouldn't go through what I went through to learn about "street credit." No one taught me about having real street credit, or the rules for money, so I wrote this to help you stay a few steps ahead of the game.

I came from a single family home. My father abandoned me when I was 3 years old and my mother was left to raise three boys by herself. I was the youngest of the three. As a single mother with no support, my mother was subjected to depend on government assistance (i.e. food stamps and welfare). I remember occasionally needing to visit the food bank at local churches. Despite my mother's hardships, she never made excuses. I learned what it meant to never give up and gained mental toughness from my mother.

In my eyes, life was normal and good. My mother was a great provider. We never went without food, clothing, or shelter. In fact, I felt we were able to keep up with the other kids and wear some of the latest fashion trends. We had cable TV, Atari, and VCR. Before the new school year started, we did a little school shopping. For Easter, we received new suits an on Christmas, new gym shoes, videos games, clothes, toys, and bikes.

My first lesson about money is a little fuzzy. All I can remember is my older brother coming home one day an asking me how much money I had in my pocket. I was 10 at the time and told him that I didn't have any. He told me that I should always have money in my pocket. That conversation with my brother stuck with me. I have had the same conversation with my own daughters. Anything my brother told me, I listened. I wanted to be just like him. He never told me how to get the money, so my imagination went to work. I knew my brother was known for having a reputation in the streets. I knew that what he was doing lead to trouble because my mom was always downtown picking him up from jail or he was being sentenced to spend time in the juvenile home.

He never allowed me to tag along much with him in those days but the few times he did, I knew he was popular. I received so much love when I was around his friends. Back then they called me Lil Codi. I imagined he sold drugs from his appearance. All the ladies wanted him. Plus, I knew the fly gear and brand-new sneakers didn't come from mom. It didn't take long for me to put two and two together that he was doing something illegal to get money.

At the age of 10, I teamed up with friends who had similar family backgrounds. We had older siblings and relatives who were selling drugs, in gangs, and had strong reputations for being cool in the streets. Naturally, this created an expectation in us to be street smart too. I was exposed to drinking, sex, and drugs at a very young age. During summer months, we chased girls, smoked weed, and had winos at the corner package store buying us 40-ounce beers and liquor. We would ride around on our dirt bikes drunk, looking for girls, and getting into trouble.

Around the sixth grade, I started selling newspapers for the *Lansing State Journal*. I liked the fact that I had a job, but disliked waking up before dawn each day to earn $10-$12 a week. So in addition to selling the newspaper, I started selling candy in school. I ended up making the same amount as the delivery job, but within a few hours! I would walk to school and before getting there stop by the corner gas station on Pleasant Grove and Holmes to purchase between $3-5 worth of Jolly Ranchers and Now & Laters. Each piece cost $.10. I would go to school and sell each pack for $.25. I turned $5 dollars into $12, making a $7 profit. I would show off at lunch and buy what I thought the kids with money purchased. See, back in those days my mother's income qualified for a school lunch ticket and with that, you had to eat the school's lunch. When I got money, I would show everyone that I could also afford to buy stuff not on the school menu, such as Hawaiian Punch, Doritos, and Little Debbie cakes.

My candy business started to generate some decent clientele and outgrew the small supply from the gas station. Instead of buying my supply from the gas station, I got my supply from a wholesaler. My competitors at school didn't have a chance now because the flavors I got from the warehouse exceeded the basic flavors they were still getting from the corner stores and gas stations. Plus I increased my profits since the cost for each piece of candy was cheaper when I bought bulk at the warehouse.

Although my friends and I picked up some bad habits from our older mentors they also showed us some positive values. Our mentors at the time all played sports and were extremely competitive and smart. I recall watching some of the best basketball players at Reo, Wainright, and Benjamin Davis Parks. I observed legends on the football field dominate Pop

Warner teams (Taylor Steelers, Southside Panthers, Kappa, and the Miller Breakers). To play a sport and not start first-string in my hometown was not cool. I also observed them working hard to be the strongest and fastest by working out and practicing on the off season. My hood also taught me to be the best at what I was doing and to do it with style. So, in addition to the bad habits we were learning in the streets, I also picked up strong work ethic, competiveness, swagger, and leadership.

By the time I made it to JW Sexton High School, I had seen and done what some adults would never experience in a lifetime. I experimented with drugs, sex, and alcohol. On the other hand, I was also known for being one of the best quarterbacks in the league. Even with a lot of negative influence going on in my environment, I never lost the ability to think and dream big.

When I started high school, I traded in candy sales for crack cocaine sales. My friends had already started selling drugs and from what I could see, they were able to get some of the expensive gear my mother wasn't able to afford. My friends' material gains tempted me to want to sell drugs too. I understood that the risk was high and could have lead me to the same traps my brother fell into. Despite the risk I believed selling dope would provide me the same advantages I seen my peers have: street creditability, money, new clothes and shoes, nice cars, jewelry, and girls. At the tender age of 13, I started selling crack cocaine and marijuana. In my mind, this was the only way to keep up with my peers. I felt I had to be as popular as my brother and have a smooth reputation with the ladies, too. My thought then was, *How will I get nice clothes, shoes, cars, an attract girls without money?* I answered my question by getting into drugs.

The same year I started high school my brother was caught distributing crack cocaine and was sentenced to five years in prison. This was a huge blow for me. The person I looked up to the most was taken away from me. I was left to figure things out alone. With no guidance, I started to make more bad choices. In addition to selling drugs, I was a heavy gambler. I started to skip class to gamble and sell drugs. The academic programs that I was awarded in middle school gradually fell off because my GPA was slipping and taking a nose dive. The only thing that kept me with a C and D average was sports. Football was my passion and I was the starting quarterback for JW Sexton Big Reds. In those days, I thought football was going to be my ticket out my neighborhood into a Division 1 college an ultimately, the NFL.

My mother and I started having problems with our relationship and I decided to move out of her home at age 16 to live with my cousin. Living at my cousin's house gave me freedom that my mother wasn't going to give. My cousin's home was clean and safe and his mother worked second shift at General Motors (GM). This was the perfect set up for two teenage boys.

My cousin's mom used to have gambling parties in her basement. All the big time high rollers were there. They would gamble through the night and morning. I witnessed 10, 20, 50, maybe even 100s of thousands of dollars being shuffled around on the crap table. I wanted some of the money on that table so bad. I remember trying to roll dice with those heavy weights an always getting beat. At the time, I was selling drugs on a regular basis, trying to balance school, and playing football.

When I was 17, there were situations that scared me straight for a few months. I was feeling a little ambitious and decided to take about thirty rocks of crack cocaine, which were worth $20 each on the block. I didn't carry all thirty at a time. I would carry about five in my hand and when I sold those, I'd go into my stash for more work. After I sold my initial five, I went to my stash and while doing so, two other young dealers ran by me and yelled, "5-0!" 5-0 was another name for the police. I immediately dropped my stash an attempted to walk up the sidewalk as if I did no wrong. The police car was coming in my direction, chasing the two others. I walked directly into the nearby community center, hoping that the cops would be gone so that I could grab my bag of dope and reconvene.

I waited for a few minutes inside and decided to walk back outside to see if the coast was clear. As I was walking toward the door to leave, two cops walked in and were headed in my direction. They quickly grabbed me, took me outside, and put me in the back of the squad car. Over-and-over I asked, "What's up? Why am I being arrested?" As I inquired, one of the cops took tweezers and removed the bag of dope that I dropped from his chest pocket. My heart dropped and my life began to flash in front of my eyes. I pleaded with the officers and told them it wasn't mine and that I was just walking from school to come to the community center, but they weren't listening.

Two years earlier, my brother was sentenced to five years for two rocks. The bag they found of mine had at least twenty-five rocks. I knew I was going to jail and for a very long time. I continued to plead with the officers, telling them the dope wasn't mine. After a long scare, the cops got out of the squad car, removed my cuffs, and told me I was free to go. Before they did, they told me they were going to fingerprint the bag later. I was distraught.

I think about that day often. I think about how much that would've hurt my mother to see another son in prison. How I would've let down my brother, family, and friends. God was with me that day. I guess the cops didn't see me drop the bag of drugs so they couldn't tie me to the dope. Whatever the reason, I thank God every day. That day made me lay low for a long time. I wanted to stay out of trouble.

High school came and went and soon enough, graduation was here. My decision to sell drugs ruined every opportunity to get selected for a football scholarship. In fact, I barely graduated. I had six hours left in my last semester of the year. Instead of having a short day like the other seniors, I had to watch over the students extra-curricular activities that took place in gym during lunch to earn extra credit. Plans for college shrunk due to my poor GPA. No college recruiters or offer letters to play college football. What a mess!

After high school, I decided to attend a junior college in Grand Rapids, MI. They had a two-year program as well as a football team that I wanted to join. The plan was to get my GPA back up, play football, and transfer to a four-year school. However, I learned that it is difficult to break bad habits. I struggled in college and began to lean on the same things I knew best: hustling and girls. Meanwhile, my older brother got out of prison from doing a five-year prison bid for selling drugs. When he got out, I decided to come back home to Lansing, MI, to help him get on his feet.

I was happy to see my brother free. I noticed a huge change in him. This time his messages to me were different. My brother began to educate me about self love, doing something for self, becoming industrious, not depending on a job but creating a job, and community development. His appearance was clean. He was cautious about what he ate. His vocabulary was unlike anything I ever heard. His posture was strong and disciplined. He was the complete opposite of how I knew him. I bet when my brother saw me he knew there was a lot of work to do to get me on track.

My brother spent time nurturing me and showing me my true value. He taught me self-improvement and community development. The literature he had me reading blew my mind. For the first time, I was being introduced to my true self, a righteous man.

We both started working at a Wendy's fast food restaurant and decided to rent a two-bedroom townhome on the south side of Lansing. Working at Wendy's was not the primary goal and we began to brainstorm ideas that would create more streams of income. I remembered that I belonged to an interest group in high school called the Omega Ladz. To raise money, we rented party halls and hosted parties. I suggested my brother and I begin renting party halls and do the same thing. My brother agreed, and we started to invest the money earned from Wendy's to start our own promotion company called Moor' Rock'n Productions. We would rent out different club houses, community centers, banquet halls, and promote parties every weekend. We charged an admissions fee at the door average $7-$10. On average, we would gross between $2500-3000 each party.

The game really changed when I learned my girlfriend was pregnant. Now the need to get money increased. In addition to promoting parties, my girlfriend's father and stepmother set me up with an interview at Electronic Data Systems (EDS). I got the job at 19 years old earning a salary of 30k per year. In addition to promoting, I now had a decent amount of income for my small family.

Thousands of dollars went through my hands. I remember buying my first sports car at 20 years old. It was a brand-new red 1997 Pontiac Grand Prix Widetrack. I remember thinking, *Wait until they see me in this.* I used to ride around with the windows down, my baseball cap backwards, and the music turned up loud, showing off. I received so much attention from everyone in that car, including the police.

I would randomly stop by the mall and buy myself and my daughter new clothes and shoes. My girlfriend and I would frequently visit our favorite restaurants. Our favorite at the time was Olive Garden restaurant. I lost and won thousands of dollars on shopping and gambling. Those were the good old days. I didn't think money would ever stop coming in. Looking back at my experiences I understand now that I was being foolish with my money and didn't have a plan.

When I turned 21, I decided to leave my job at EDS and start my own business. People thought I was crazy but the do-for-self lectures my brother used to give me were embedded in my mind. To work my entire life for someone else was not an option. In addition to everything else I was doing, I became interested in selling fine oils, lotions, scented candles, and incense. I would look for opportunities to vend my products at festivals. Then I got the idea to set up a kiosk within the local mall. I figured, instead of waiting for periodic festivals to vend my products, a kiosk at the mall would give me the consistency I needed to make money daily. I used all the pennies I had saved up to put down a deposit for rent and purchase inventory. A friend loaned me a few extra dollars to pay the rent up a few months to give me cushion. After everything was settled, I was open for business.

Meanwhile, my brother and I still promoted parties and I still had a few other hustles on the side. The kiosk did ok for a while and it made me feel good because I had some form of pride of ownership and support for my family. At age 22, I owned my own business and gave birth to another precious baby girl. Business began to slow down and several of the anchor stores in the mall closed. As a result, the flow of traffic dissipated. The mall rent combined with the slow traffic became stressful. Eventually, the cost exceeded profits and I had to shut down.

After closing my kiosk, my life took a devastating turn. Things got extremely tough when I learned that my brother passed away. Everything happened so fast. I received a phone call from authorities who were at my mother's home. I could tell by the woman's voice that something was wrong. I didn't know what it was, but knew it involved my brother. I didn't let her continue. I quickly got in the car and rushed to my mother's home. The police were there and my mother was sitting in her chair crying. I walked towards her and she told me the painful news that my brother was dead. I couldn't cry because I wanted to be strong for her and be in control of the situation. The first thing I did was kneel on the ground, hugged my mom, and worked to absorb all the pain. I just hugged her tight. I didn't want her to be harmed. I only wanted to take away any pain that she was feeling.

In that moment of grief, pain, and disbelief, God sent me a guardian angel to give me some peace of mind. My friend who was there with me told me, "I may have lost one brother but you've gained one more." For some reason, that touched my heart and comforted me. I was overwhelmed, yet I instantly felt better. His words helped me to regain the strength I needed to push forward.

The streets we depended on were the same streets that took his life. The feeling I felt when I learned of his death is difficult to relive. After his death, I was motivated to make some positive changes. I married my children's mother and gave myself totally to God. After mourning the death of my brother, I got motivated to pick myself back up and continue what we both started, which was promoting events.

My wife and I used our kitchen at home to supply lunch and dinners to salon owners around town. After a few months, the money saved was enough to make some investments. At the time there were no outlets for young people and I decided to open up a teen night club in my brother's honor called, Club Bicos. Bico was my brother's middle name. In the beginning, the club did well, but the kids started to lose interest. Partygoers dwindled after 6 months. When I figured out how to fix the problem it was too late I was out of money and had to shut down.

I've come to appreciate all of my experiences in my neighborhood. The time spent with my childhood friends, mentors and coaches are priceless. The experiences that created a pivotal shift in my thinking the most were the many talks my brother and I had about doing for self. I have a deep appreciation and love for him. In many ways, I believe God used him to save my life. I also had some eye opening conversations when my kiosk was in business at the mall.

Many people from different walks of life used to stopped by and converse with me. They were amazed at my age and how I was an owner of my own store. While they were praising me, I thought to myself that they just didn't know that my other homeboys across town also had retail stores. I recall having a conversation with a few people and discussing how youth didn't learn about money, money management, or credit in school. I realized they were right because I was one of those students who didn't have financial literacy.

It is due to those experiences that I am writing this book. I founded Street Credit Incorporated for you. I want to prevent youth from repeating the same mistakes I made and get youth started early to gain financial freedom. The time is now. In the following chapters, I will highlight key principles and strategies that you can implement immediately to set yourself up for a lifestyle of your choice and earn real Street Credit.

May God bless you with the light of understanding. Pass it on. Peace!

Questions to Ask Yourself

What do you want to know about money?

_____
_____
_____
_____

When do you think you should start learning about money?

_____
_____

Why is it important to learn money management?

_____
_____
_____
_____

What is wealth?

_____
_____

What is financial freedom?

_____
_____

What is money management?

_____
_____

Questions to ask your Parents, Teachers, & Mentors

How did you learn about money?

_____

_____

_____

Where did you learn about the rules to the money game?

_____

_____

_____

How do you keep track of your money?

_____

_____

_____

What does financial freedom mean to you?

_____

_____

_____

Do you have any investments?

_____

What are you doing to prepare for retirement?

_____

_____

_____

What are you doing to prepare for my education?

_____

_____

_____

What would change if you could start over financially?

_____

_____

_____

Street Cred:

An Introduction

When you think about the term, street credit, what comes to mind? If you have a similar background as mine, you may think of someone from your neighborhood who has a strong reputation. The person you may have in mind is typically known for being hard, tough, and doesn't take any mess from anyone. Unfortunately, this person has talent, but is not known for having academic success. In most cases, they have a criminal background. This person has a reputation for making money by selling drugs or other risky hustles. They have all the hood rich items i.e. the latest clothes, shoes, cars, friends, and girls. They are natural leaders and have many followers; however, their paths lead to lifestyles of violence, jail, and an early grave.

This book is intended to give you the true definition of street credit. This book offers instructions that will lead you to a lifestyle of prosperity and wealth. Not only will you achieve street credibility on your block, or hood, but you will learn principles that will give you influence over cities as well as states. In fact, if your game is tight you will learn to have influence over the entire world!

Depending on how you think, influencing the world may seem to be far from reality. Why does becoming a global-international player seem far-fetched to you? If you think this is impossible, what caused you to think less of yourself? I am here to tell you that you are bigger than your block, city, or hood. You were born to succeed and influence humanity! Someone has to do it. Why not you?

As you build wealth, your foundation must be strong. Before you can receive wealth, you need a wealthy mindset. Without having a true love for self, you become a walking liability rather than an asset. As discussed, you spend precious time and resources impressing people you do not know.

Self-love is the foundation needed to ensure you have the proper street credit. When you begin to receive your riches without having self-love, you will begin to use your money in a self-defeating manner. You will look for things on the outside to build your self-worth. Many who have low self-esteem utilize their money to buy things to build their exterior shell. For example, you will see people buying expensive clothing, cars, and jewelry all to impress strangers. At the same time, they are struggling to maintain the things used to create a false perception of who they really are. This is why self-love is critical. There won't be a need to use money to buy material things to make you feel valuable. No need to waste money on things to impress others. People will be impressed by your walk, your spirit, and the attitude you possess. Everything added on to the outside will be icing on the cake.

Without self-love, life can be expensive and in some cases, bad for your health. Many who do not love themselves to the degree in which they should, find material items or addictions to help them to cope. There is nothing wrong with material items, but if you use these things to help you feel better about yourself, it can become a problem. When you don't have a strong foundation, you can develop addictions to cigarettes, alcohol, drugs, sex, or overeating which will all have you spending unnecessary money. Vices such as these will suck the life from you and suffocate your resources. They keep you in a perpetual state of want, struggle, and dissatisfaction all the days of your life.

> *Nothing outside of self should validate who you are.*

Before you move forward, understand that in order for you to have true street credit, you have to have true self-love. Love for self simply means that you know your value and will protect and give yourself the best that this life has to offer. Nothing outside of self should validate who you are. Everything that validates you comes from your soul, your essence, and your being. When you value, know, and love self, you feel good, walk with your shoulders back, and have your head lifted. This is the first step to having street credit!

> *The next chapter will discuss the first law needed to build wealth. Pay close attention to this chapter because it is the key ingredient to making sure you have the swagger to handle the position of having street credit.*

Notes

Know Thyself/Love for Self

The first rule for having street credit is to love yourself first. When I say love yourself, I mean much more than an emotional feeling.   This means you know your worth and will do everything within your control to provide the best this planet has to offer. Self love can vary from person to person. As your love increases your expectations and choices change.

The type of foods you eat, friends, people you attract, places you go, and music you listen to will change. As your love for self expands, you begin to realize that you deserve more than the best. As your love increases, you begin to realize that you're bigger than your hood, city, or state. This elevated state of mind equips us with the mental capacity to understand that we deserve the best because we are the best. When you have self-love, you love God. The connection is made that you are a child of God and the entire universe is your inheritance.

> *To love self means to value who you are as a person.*

When building wealth, your foundation must be strong. Before you can receive wealth, you have to possess a wealthy mindset. Your self-love secures you as an asset rather than a liability. You will not misuse time or resources to impress people you don't know. Instead, your foundation will ensure you have the proper street credit, or financial swagger, to build prosperity.

Understand that without a secure foundation, you will continuously defeat yourself. This creates low self-esteem, which will lead you to use money in a self-defeating manner. Your money will become your definition of worth. For example, some people will buy expensive clothes, cars, or jewelry as an expression of their worth.

Therefore, self-love is the first law of wealth. Love for self builds one's self-worth while acknowledging one's value. When you understand your worth, you will not settle for less. You begin to attract who you are. As your self-love increases, your expectations

> *Change begins within and transforms those things outside.*

and choices change. The types of food you eat, your friends, people you attract, places you go, even the music you groove to will have to change.

Change begins within and transforms those things outside. Once your level of self-worth rises, your expectations will follow. You will realize that your value is not in material things. You will expect more from yourself and others. You will realize you're bigger than your "block." Know that you are more than the human eye can see. You were created to master this universe.

"Change begins within and transforms those things outside."

Companies use a process called SWOT to identify important things about themselves and their external environment. We can also conduct a personal SWOT for the same reason. SWOT stands for:

S = Strengths

W = Weakness

O = Opportunities

T = Threats

Strengths – What advantages or gifts do you have?

Weakness – What can you improve?

Opportunities – What good opportunities can you spot?

Threats – What obstacles do you face?

S.W.O.T.
Analysis

Take a moment to list your internal strengths and weaknesses as well as external opportunities and threats.

Strengths:	Weakness
1. Athletic	1. Math
2. Math	2. Overeating
3. Sing/Rap	3. Study Habits
4. Public Speaking	4. Focus
5. Speed	5. Technical Skills
6.	6.
7.	7.
8.	8.
9.	9.
10.	10.
Opportunities	**Threats**
1. Tutoring Program	1. Transportation
2. After School Programs	2. Weather
3. Coaches/Mentors	3. Lack of money
4. Good Weather	4. No Internet
5. Uncut Lawns	5. Negative Relationships
6.	6.
7.	7.
8.	8.
9.	9.
10.	10.

Notes

Do You Have a Hustle?

Knowing who you are, your strengths, and weaknesses is the second law to having street credit. Once you know who you are, it is your responsibility to use your God-given gifts to get money! Everyone is good at something. Discover what you are good at and get to work!

Unfortunately, it takes some of us longer than others to discover our strengths and begin creating money. The people who are close to us should bring out the best in us but sometimes that is not always the case. In today's society, parents are too busy working and trying to provide for their children rather than spending time with them. Extracurricular activities, such as reading, writing, sports, music, and arts and crafts are beginning to fall to the wayside, while technology consumes our time. Seldom are parents able to have meaningful conversations at dinner to stimulate dialogue to get children thinking about harnessing their strengths. Schools are becoming monotonous and robotic.

You are being prepared to learn how to memorize material for a test as opposed to discovering your strengths and learning how to relate those strengths to the real world. In most cases, schools have proven to be counterproductive when a child doesn't pass a test. The child often feels inadequate, defeated, and misdiagnosed as being dumb or stupid. The truth is that these tests have very little to do with pulling out who you really are. In fact, if some of the richest people in the world today were to take those same tests, they would probably fail. Does that mean they're stupid? Not at all.

My suggestion is that you find someone you trust who is headed toward where you want to be in life. Mentorship is a great way to beef up your skills and receive feedback about your progress from someone who truly cares. In most cases, a mentor will not be a parent or a sibling but a close friend of the family, a relative, the owner of the corner store, a coach, the

> *Find someone you trust who is headed toward where you want to be in life.*

neighborhood mechanic, senior class president, pastor, and or bus driver. Contrary to what most people believe, everyone likes to share. No successful person got to where they are in life alone. Who was Jay Z's mentor(s)? What about Russell Simmons, Steve Jobs, Albert Einstein, Barack Obama, Malcolm X, and Oprah Winfrey? If we interviewed these great giants, they would all list names of people who they borrowed and learned from to strengthen their skills.

I challenge you to get outside of your normal circle of influence and find someone who you would like to learn from and build a relationship. And it's ok to have several mentors. I recommend that you do. Be honest with who you choose by letting them know that you admire their work ethic and that you would like their help. If you approach someone with a sincere heart to learn, they will be glad to take you under their wing. I know what you're saying, "Most people are too busy." I said that to my mentor one day and she said, "If you want to get something done, *always* ask a busy person." Surround yourself with people you want to be like. Remember this, if you hang with five broke friends you are more than likely the sixth one.

My mentor also told me that the exposure you receive from a good coach can sometimes be more valuable than the training we receive at school. Learn your strengths and what value you add to society. After discovering your strengths and the uniqueness you have been blessed with, begin finding ways to use those talents to create money.

Here are a few examples:

1. Math tutor
2. Personal trainer
3. Landscaping
4. Babysitting
5. Sell candy
6. Barber
7. Beautician
8. Create an art gallery and sell art
9. Become a writer
10. Create a popular blog site (good content sells)
11. Create a YouTube channel

DO YOU HAVE A HUSTLE?

Notes

Thinking of a Master Plan

Everyone seems to want to be rich or wealthy. On my financial literacy tours, I ask students the question, *Who would like to be rich or wealthy one day?* Most times, every hand in the class goes up. I believe if we asked our parents, relatives, friends, and neighbors the same question their hands would also go up. Many people believe that money equates to happiness, but that isn't always true. However, many stresses of the world are created because of a lack of money. I heard my mentor say, "money can't buy happiness, but it sure is a good down payment."

Before moving further, I want you to take out a sheet of paper. At the top, write the word: Wealthy. Without looking in a dictionary try your best to define this word. Next, I want you to think of few people who you think might be wealthy. After you develop your list, write down some possible descriptions of their lifestyle. Here is an example: Beyoncé – happy, beautiful, easy going, popular, free.

I'm going to ask you the same question I ask my students, "Do you want to be wealthy?" I am willing to bet that the answer is yes. As I stated earlier, most people respond the same way. Most people want to have money and plenty of it. Some of the words you used to describe the wealthy are beautiful. We all deserve that same lifestyle or better. Don't let anyone tell you different.

By now, you have seen some of the traps and pitfalls of life. You have been exposed to what a little education, homelessness, unemployment, hunger, and a down economy can produce. A lack of money is the leading cause of crime, divorce, and other hardships that create an uncomfortable lifestyle. Never believe that life is easy without money. That is a lie. Money gives you the ability to be free—freedom to do what you were created to do. Plenty of money and resources will give you the ability to help your fellow man. Without money, you will be in a position of servitude, and wishing you had the means to do this or that.

> *A lack of money is the leading cause of crime, divorce, and other hardships that create an uncomfortable lifestyle.*

Earlier we discussed knowing yourself and your strengths. It pleases God for you to utilize your strengths to produce your needs and wants. Even strange beasts, animals, and insects understand their strengths and use them. So why should you do differently? You are God's best creation. Enjoy heaven on earth as it is in heaven. Amen.

Most will agree that money will help them to live their desired lifestyle but the truth is that very few people know how to create that lifestyle. While one-hundred percent of Americans agree that they want to be rich, right now seventy-five percent are living paycheck-to-paycheck. What does this statistic teach? It shows that people want wealth but don't know how to obtain it.

"right now **75%** are living paycheck-to-paycheck."

There is a famous quote that I like and it says, "People don't plan to fail. They fail to plan." Read that quote aloud. I don't know why but it always twists up my tongue. What does that mean to you? Think about it, "People don't plan to fail. They fail to plan." One-hundred percent of people want to be wealthy, but seventy-five percent or more never achieve that goal. Why? You got it! They didn't have a plan.

According to the statistics, only one out of four Americans have enough savings to cover monthly expenses for six months for crisis situations like job loss, medical expenses, or other unexpected accidents. Roughly three-quarters of Americans are living paycheck-to-paycheck. Paycheck-to-paycheck means before a person can cash their check it is already spent on bills. After that paycheck is spent there isn't any money left. They are without money until their next check comes. This is a vicious cycle; it's an uncomfortable, unfulfilling lifestyle. This is unfair for a person to work a part-time or full-time schedule and before they can enjoy the fruits of their labor it is

> *People don't plan to fail. They fail to plan.*

spent on bills. Nothing is left over to save, invest, or enjoy.

Take out that same sheet of paper from earlier. Now list 5-10 people you know who live paycheck-to-paycheck. After listing their names, write a list of adjectives that describe their lifestyle.

Here are some examples of adjectives:

stressed, unhappy, tired, worried, and depressed

Compare your list and decide which lifestyle you want to live. I'm glad you choose to be wealthy. Now the question is, How does one become wealthy?

Unfortunately, the people you know who live this paycheck-to-paycheck lifestyle were mis-educated. They were taught to go to school, get good grades, graduate, go to college, and find a good job. You have probably been taught the same. Do you know the definition of insanity? The definition is trying the same thing over-and-over expecting a different result. That is precisely what we are doing. We all get taught the same stuff in school. However, the majority of the people who use this map lead to a lifestyle that causes them to live paycheck-to-paycheck. By no means am I suggesting not to do your best in school, get good grades, and move forward to college. What I am suggesting is that there are some missing pages to this map. These missing pages teach us how to use our education to become wealthy and gain financial freedom.

One other myth is that you can achieve wealth by saving money. This couldn't be further from the truth. Saving is important and has its purpose but it has never been a formula that leads people to wealth or financial freedom. People usually never have enough to save or end up dipping into their saving to use it for various needs and wants.

Pay close attention to the following chapters. What I will share with you next are the missing pages that are not taught in your school textbooks. The information I am going to give you will be the blueprint you need to create wealth as well as a desired lifestyle. I will expose you to secrets that the wealthy use to acquire and maintain financial freedom.

> *The better you know the rules of the game, the better your chances are to win.*

Every game has rules. The better you know the rules of the game, the better your chances are to win. Life, ladies and gentleman, is a game. The more you understand the rules of the game will dictate your quality of life. Take a second and think. Who taught you about money? Where did you learn your first lesson about money? Is the person you learned about money wealthy or living paycheck-to-paycheck? Just like my story, many of you don't know who taught you about money. Or, the person you're learning from doesn't know much, either. How do you expect to learn the game if you don't have a good teacher?

I wrote this book to share with you what I have learned about the game and give you the missing links they are not teaching us at home or in school. This may come as a shock to some of you, but I have to break the news to you anyway. You cannot

> *Wishing and hoping for wealth is a waste of time.*

get rich by playing the lottery. Poor people waste millions each year playing games of chance. Wishing and hoping for wealth is waste of time. Instead of gambling our lives away, we are going to take control of our lives and destiny. We are going to use our God-given gifts and talents to place ourselves in heaven. Not by chance, but because we are going to understand the rules to game.

Moving forward, I am going to refer to those living paycheck-to-paycheck as the "seventy five percent" and people who have financial freedom as the "twenty-five percent."

The difference between the two is simple: One knows the rules of the game and the other doesn't. The seventy-five percent believe they need to find a job, earn a paycheck, and try to save, save, save. But that never happens. That seldom works. Once they receive that paycheck, their money has one job and that is to spend. The wealthy know that money is not used for spending. They know how to flip their earned income into an asset to create more money. We will talk about assets later. The wealthy believe in one principle and that principle is to pay yourself first.

"One knows the rules of the game and the other doesn't..."

Notes

"GET READY TO START THE GAME"

Get Ready to Start the Game

For starters, you must have a hustle that will create income. Next, get ready to put your old shoe boxes in your closet to use. You will need six boxes that will be used to store money. At this point, you should have listed your strengths and know what you're good at doing. Now it's up to you to be creative and determine how to leverage your God-given gifts and talents to get your hustle on and create money. Once you have your hustle(s) in place, you are ready to start the game and fill up your 6 shoe boxes.

Filling up the boxes is only one part of the game. In the next chapter, I will describe the rules for each box and how to play and win the game. Each shoe box has a name and specific purpose and will be used to store your monthly income. In the following chapters, I will describe the specific rules for each box and help you understand what money goes inside, as well as the rules to follow when taking money out. Pay close attention to the rules. The more you understand the rules of the game the more likely you will beat out your opponents and win!

Notes

Box 1:
Skills to Pay the Bills
(Living Expenses)

Rule: *Use this box only for monthly household needs to maintain your lifestyle.*

The first shoe box is dedicated to your monthly household budget. Label this box *"Living Expenses."* Monthly living costs vary and will be different depending on a person's chosen lifestyle. Here is also where most people get into the biggest trouble financially. Monthly expenses should only be those things that are needed to maintain your lifestyle every month. The problem is that seventy-five percent of Americans live outside their means and increase their monthly expenses by using credits cards, taking out high interest loans, and using those cards and loans to purchase liabilities. Basically, the seventy-five percent have too much money going out and not enough money coming in.

EXERCISE - NEED OR WANT?

In this exercise, you will need to determine which of the following items listed are needs or wants.

Needs	Need or Want?
Groceries	
Movies	
Eating out	
Mortgage/Rent	
Shoes, clothes	
Energy Bill	
Credit Card Bill	
Daycare	
Candy bar	
The Club	
Video Game	

If you take a look at the examples, needs are those things you must pay every month to live. If they are not paid, you may receive a penalty in the game. Those penalties can be costly and may lead to eviction notices, disconnection notices, starvation, and late payments that can result in debt or bad credit. Wants are those things that you don't need and can live without. If you don't buy a want there is no penalty. Be careful because wants have a tendency to consume most of our money and is the main cause for a person not having enough money for their needs. This eventually leads to a poor and stressful lifestyle of living paycheck-to-paycheck.

After you have made your list, make sure you go back to review. Look at your list carefully as if you were a CEO or President of a major firm. One of the primary jobs of a business owner is to protect the bottom line. In other words, make sure that all expenses going out are necessary. If you see something that isn't a need, slide it over into the wants column.

Our list can become very long on both sides. The primary goal and objective are to identify those things you really don't need and put them in their proper place. While playing the Money Game, this will help you to see where you're wasting your bread, or money. This exercise will also show you how credit cards and loans turn into long-term debt that can become too expensive to pay.

The wants we can't afford are sometimes purchased with a credit card or loans. When you take out loans or credit cards to purchase a want, it becomes a monthly obligation that must be paid within the agreed amount of time. However, when you repay the debt, an interest rate is associated with that payment. Sometimes the rate of interest can range between 0-29% and higher depending upon an individual credit score.

A good rule to follow is if you can't pay cash for it, you can't afford it! Borrowing money and using credit cards to make purchases is dangerous. If we really understood the real cost for borrowing money; and add up all the interest they pay overtime on loans and credit cards they would be shocked.

Creditors make it easy to get a credit card but they don't make it easy for consumers to fully understand the terms and fees for making late payments; or the real cost to pay off the debt overtime.

"DON'T GO BROKE TRYING TO LOOK RICH. ACT YOUR WAGE!"

Donald wants a new flat screen television that cost $1000. He doesn't have $1000 cash and decided to charge the television on his credit card. Donald has two options:

1. Pay cash for the television.
2. Use credit card and make monthly payments until the flat screen television is paid in full.

Since Donald is choosing to use a credit card the cost of the TV will be more expensive. The minimum payment required will be $20 per month with an interest rate of 18%.

If Donald makes the minimum payment of $20 at a rate of 18%, it will take him 8 years to pay off this debt. Well, after 8 years the flat screen TV won't be new anymore, and the price will have doubled.

Estimated cost   **$2,000**

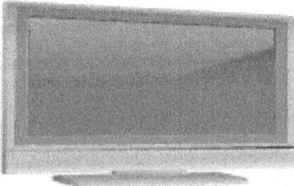

These basic problems illustrate how one purchase can end up costing much more over time when using loans or credit cards. When playing the Money Game to win, this can be a slippery slope because if you make late payments, you can receive costly penalties or fines.

The more debt you add, the more your monthly obligation will be. The more expenses you have, the more money you have going out. Also the more you have to pay, the more you're forced to work. Debt is slavery. The objective of the Money Game is to get financially free, not get into debt (slavery).

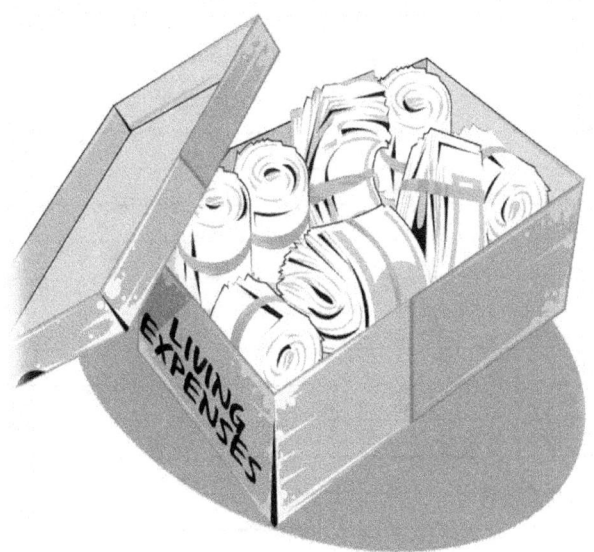

Notes

Box 2:
Don't Get Caught Slip'n (Savings)

Rule: Use box for emergencies and large purchases over $100.

The next box is for emergencies and large purchases. Label this box "savings." While playing the Money Game, this box is vital. If your game is going to be tight, you can't get caught slipping. The way to avoid slipping is to have a savings stash. Many who lose the game fail because they lack to understand this essential rule.

Many also make the mistake and believe that saving money is how they will become financially free. This box is essential to you winning the game but this box function is not financial freedom. The purpose of this box is to get you out of a jam when life throws you a few challenges along the way or when it's time to make a large purchase. Do you remember my favorite quote, "People don't plan to fail, they fail to plan?" CEO's and presidents of major corporations understand that life happens and things don't always go as planned. However, if you prepare for those things before they happen you can get through them much easier.

Companies who are here today and gone tomorrow are not good at forecasting trouble. People who fail at this part of the game take an unrealistic approach to life and don't prepare for those rainy days that are sure to come. The better you are at forecasting profits and losses, the longer you and your business will survive. This principle is used in business but don't forget that you too are a business. The same strategies used in businesses should be used and applied at home and in our personal lives.

The other function this box is used for includes large purchases. Large purchases are inevitable. Why? Once again, most people get caught slipping because they don't plan ahead for these large purchases. Rather than plan, they take out loans and use credit cards to make the purchase not realizing that those same loans and credit cards will get them closer to debt (slavery) and further away from financial freedom.

Let's take a few minutes and learn the real use for this box.

EXERCISE – DON'T GET CAUGHT SLIP'N

Take out a separate piece of paper and label the paper, "Savings: Don't Get Caught Slip'n." Create two columns and label one, "Emergencies," and the other, "Large Purchases (Anything over $100)". In the Emergencies column, list specific emergences that can occur. In the other column, list large purchases that cost over $100 that we will need to buy in our lifetime. The more specific you are, the better. See the table below for a few examples:

Emergencies	Large Purchases
Flat tire	New/Used Car
Plumbing issues	TV
Broken window	Vacation
Lawyer fees	Wedding
Unemployment	College

Maybe not all the emergencies will happen to you in your lifetime but I guarantee a few things on that list will. At some point, you may need a lawyer, lose your job, need car repair, or have to fix a window. The same goes for making large purchases. All of us plan to buy a home, purchase a new car, or take a vacation. I f w e know that these things will come to pass, what are we waiting for? Is the money going to fall out the sky? No! We have to start setting aside a stash to get ready now. However, those who get caught slipping don't plan, don't prepare, and don't save.

The seventy-five percent go along day-to-day as if these things are never going to happen. Then all of the sudden, *SMASH!* They get into a car accident; need a lawyer, or funds to pay a traffic fine. Where will they get the money to pay? Instead of getting out of their "Don't Get Caught Slip'n" stash, they use quick fixes that turn into long-term debt such as bothering family and friends for money or taking out high interest loans and credit cards. Both increase debt and get you closer to slavery—not financial freedom.

> *Those who get caught slipping don't plan, don't prepare, and don't save.*

A frequent question is asked about how much should be stashed away in savings. Most financial gurus recommend you have at least 6 to 12 months of your monthly living expenses stashed away at minimum. I say, shoot for 12 months. It's good to always forecast a rainy day. If you lose your job today, will you still be able to maintain your lifestyle and pay all of your monthly obligations? It's sad but we learn every day on the news of how people get laid-off from their jobs and cannot find a replacement job. They end up using what little stash they had, if any, and then fall behind on their monthly obligations and bills. When you fall behind fines and penalties come. "The Man" doesn't want any excuses, either. If you don't pay what is required, you will be evicted from your home. Your lights, heat, and phone will be cut off, and your car will be repossessed. When you don't have a savings stashed away for tough times, your world can be turned upside down and inside out.

EXERCISE – MAINTAINING THE LIFESTYLE

Earlier you made a list of monthly needs that help you to maintain your lifestyle. On that same list, give each item a dollar amount. Once you have associated the cost for each expense, calculate the total.

For example,

Monthly Expenses $1200 x 6 Months = $7200

Monthly Expenses $1200 x 12 Months = $14400

Total Monthly Expenses

Total Monthly Expenses _____X 6 Months =_____

Total Monthly Expenses _____X 12 Months =_____

The number total for 6 months or 12 months is a good amount to have stashed in your "Don't Get Caught Slip'n Box. The more the merrier so if you can find ways to exceed your savings goal then by all means do so. Players and successful business men/women who do well preparing for rainy days don't get caught slipping.

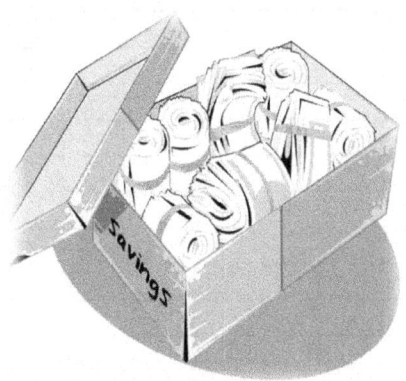

Notes

Assets vs. Liabilities

Before we move forward to the other shoe boxes, I want to take a few minutes to discuss the difference between assets and liabilities. Learning the difference between the two will help you to understand how the rich continue to get richer and the poor continues to get poorer. Knowing the difference between the two will ensure your game is tight and earn you superior street creditability.

To put it simply, wealthy people make it a habit to spend their money on assets and poor people have a habit of spending their money on liabilities. Wealthy people know that acquiring more assets will create more money and make them financially free. On the other hand, poor people think what they buy has value but the things they purchase puts them further in debt, which keeps them in a state of perpetual slavery.

Knowing the difference between liabilities and

> **Assets put money into your pocket and liabilities take money out.**

assets is simple. Assets put money *into* your pocket and liabilities take money *out*. Although the differences are clear, our vision can be blurred by the powerful influence of the media and peers who make us believe something has value when it really doesn't. In order to win the game, you must know the difference. Your ability to acquire more assets over liabilities is the key to financial freedom.

EXERCISE - SPENDING

Number a sheet of paper from 1-10. Create a list of 10 things you spend your money on. After you have spent some time writing down things you buy, create two columns. Label the first column, "Assets" and the second column, "Liabilities."

Look at your list and categorize your purchases into the Assets or Liabilities columns.

Remember the rule as you categorize:

Assets put money into your pocket while Liabilities takes money out your pocket. See example below and discuss.

Purchases	Assets	Liabilities
Shoes	Stocks	Shoes
Clothes	Truck	Clothes
Hair Salon	Hair Salon	Car
Car		
Truck		
Cell Phone		
House		

Now that you have your list of assets and liabilities, you should be able to see what puts money in your pocket and what takes money away. If you noticed some items could go in either column. For example, truck or a house could be considered an asset or a liability. Depending on how these two items are used will make the difference. Remember the rule: An asset puts money *into* your pocket, while a liability takes money *out* your pocket. Using this rule we could quickly assume that a truck and a house take money out your pocket. However, let's put on our business hats and flip these liabilities into assets.

EXERCISE: CONVERTING LIABILITIES INTO ASSETS

Take a few minutes review the following liabilities that have been turned into assets. Then, determine how the next set of liabilities can become assets.

1. *Truck*
   Asset: A truck can be used for moving furniture or trash.

2. *House*
   Asset: A house can be used as a daycare facility.

   Now let's see if you can convert the next set of liabilities into assets.

   1. *Computer*
      Asset:

      _____

      _____.

   2. *Shoe collection*
      Asset:

      _____

      _____

   3. *Cell phone*

      Asset:

      _____

      _____

For starters, the majority of us may have learned that our liability column is longer than the one for assets. The key to wealth is shortening our liabilities and extending our assets. Making the transition from valuing assets over liabilities requires a change in personal values. There must be a paradigm shift from a consumer mindset to having a boss mindset. You cannot value cars, clothes, jewelry, fancy bags, and shoes more than you do investments in assets. Moving forward, before you reach into your pockets to spend, ask yourself one simple question. Say, "Self, is this purchase going to make me money or take money away?" The formula to wealth is simple: The more assets you acquire, the more money you will create. The more liabilities you acquire the less money you'll make.

> *The more assets you acquire, the more money you will create. The more liabilities you acquire the less money you'll make.*

Now that you know better, it's your responsibility to do better. If your game is really tight and you want to win the money game moving forward, make sure you acquire more assets than liabilities.

There is nothing wrong with having nice things. I believe if you want it you should get it. However, there is a correct way about getting what you want. The mistake poor people make is that they buy a liability first. Wealthy people do the exact opposite. They buy an asset first, which creates more money to buy the liability that they want. In another instance, the poor will buy a new car without creating additional income to support the new car. On the flip side, wealthy people will first invest in an asset, produce more money, then purchase a new car. The system the wealthy use is simple. They create more cash flow before they add more expenses. They add more assets before adding more liabilities. Poor people add more expenses without increasing their cash flow, which causes them to drown in debt.

Notes

Box 3:
Scared Money
Don't Make Money
(Investments)

Rule: Use the money in this box when you are going to make more money.

Now that you have learned a little about assets and liabilities, it's time to learn about the most important box called, the Investment box. Label this box "investments." I like to call it "Scared Money Don't Make Money." While learning about the rules for this box, you will begin to understand why it is so important to know the difference between assets, liabilities and taking risks. If you use this box correctly, you will no longer need to earn your income. Instead, you will master the art of creating income. What's the difference? I thought you'd ask.

Earned income is how most people make their money. Before you get paid, you have to do something for an agreed amount of time. Some people flip burgers for 8 hrs per day, cut hair, work on an assembly line, or a corporate office. There are several things people do to earn income. Let me go on the record by saying there is nothing wrong with earning a living and having a career if that's what you choose to do. However, there is a difference between choosing to work and being forced to work to keep up with your lifestyle. Imagine what it would be like to choose to work rather than be forced. Being forced to work is a form of modern-day slavery. This box will give you control and power over your life and give you the freedom to choose what you want to do with your life.

Instead of depending on earned income you must set up passive income. Some people also call it residual income or portfolio income. It can create money for you, regardless of where you are. Unlike earned income, passive income is unique. Passive income pays you while you are on vacation, asleep, visiting friends, or sitting around the house. Author Robert Kiyosaki designed a chart that illustrates the difference between people who earn income and people who create income. The chart was created to show the difference in mindset between the wealthy and the poor. Kiyosaki also believes that it is difficult to become financially free trading your time for earned income. The truth is you can never become financially free with only earned income. You must step your game up and learn the power of turning your earned income into passive income.

> **Two Income Types:**
>
> **Earned**
> **&**
> **Passive**

Kiyosaki explained two philosophies of learning in his book, *Rich Dad Poor Dad*. He explained that his poor dad believed getting a good education and finding a good job was the key to success. However, his rich dad had a different perspective. His rich dad believed you don't work for money you make money work for you. Below is an illustration called the Cash Flow Quadrant designed by Kiyosaki. He teaches that the left side of the quadrant was his poor dad's values and the right side is his rich dad's values. Make note of the differences. Which side do you want to be on?

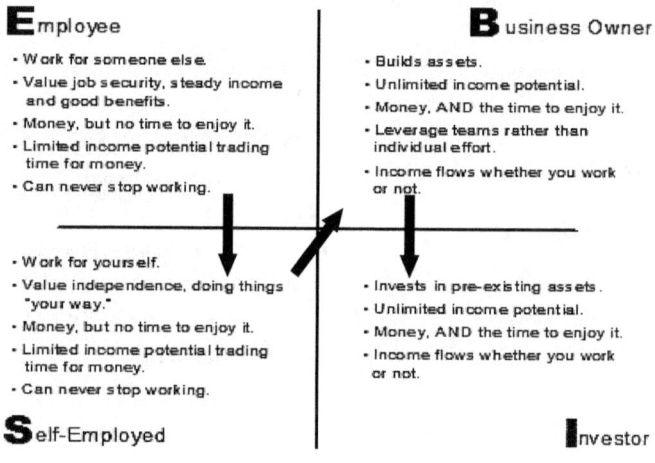

Diagram from the book, Rich Dad Poor Dad by Robert Kiyosaki

The areas on the left side of the quadrant (employee & self-employed) are persons who work hard and trade time for money. In addition, the left side seldom has time to enjoy their money. The common feature on the right side of the quadrant (business & investor) is that they invest in assets to create money, and they have time to enjoy their money.

There is nothing wrong with either side but if your goal is financial freedom, it will be difficult to achieve this status by only receiving earned income. The key to wealth and financial freedom is investing in assets and creating multiple streams of income.

The wealthy invest money in three areas to create money. Those three areas are with real estate, business, and stocks. Wealthy people know that the more they acquire these three assets the more money they will

> *The key to wealth and financial freedom is investing in assets and creating multiple streams of income.*

create. Earlier we discussed the difference between an assets and liabilities. The formula to wealth is not complex. You must learn to value and acquire assets over liabilities. It's easy to remember the difference between an asset and liability. Remember to ask yourself one question, "Will this purchase make me money or take money away?" If your purchase is going to make you more money, it is an asset. If the purchase takes money away it is a liability. See the following three assets:

Real Estate – Property that consists of houses and land

Business – An organization or economic system where goods and services are exchanged for one another or money

Stock – A share of a company held by an individual or a group.

Real estate is a great way to create wealth. Imagine if you owned land, several homes, apartment buildings, and office buildings and the tenants paid you a fee/rent to live or operate their businesses. How about purchasing homes, apartment complexes, or commercial buildings under market value? You fix them up and sell them for more than what you paid. Real estate is a perfect way to create tons of extra cash flow and gain access to financial freedom.

Starting and owning a business is another cool way the wealthy achieve financial freedom. The reward for having a unique idea and manifesting that idea into reality is wealth. Every place we shop and spend our money started first as an idea in someone's head. If we turn back the hands of time we will notice that every business had a humble beginning, started small, and progressed to the top over time. Before McDonalds became a multibillion dollar company and a leader in the fast food industry they had a very humble beginning.

The restaurant idea started in 1937 by Patrick J. MacDonald. He opened a small food stand called, "The Airdrome." He sold hamburgers for .10 cents each. In 1940, his sons Richard and Maurice McDonald picked up the baton, renamed the business "McDonalds Bar-B-Q" and sold BBQ items. In 1948, the McDonald's brothers realized the majority of their success came from selling hamburgers. They decided to simplify their menu and only sell .15 cent hamburgers, fries, shakes, and soft drinks. The two brothers changed the name again to "McDonalds" and the rest is history. By 1960, McDonalds had 1000 locations. In 2011, it's been reported that there were 31,000 McDonald's locations worldwide and reached $27 Billion.

Earlier, I discussed the importance of loving self and knowing your strengths. The difference between the wealthy and poor is that the wealthy act on their ideas. Every idea may not make you the first million but like the McDonald's family, you must take risks, be patient, evaluate, and make necessary changes. In addition, you must not be afraid to fail. What if the McDonalds brothers did not act on their idea? What if the McDonalds brothers gave up when times got tough? Well, I'll tell you what would've happened. Someone else with more courage, toughness, and patience would have kept going and took their fortune. You must believe in yourself. When times get tough, hang in there.

Burgers might not be your thing, but it's your responsibility to find your niche. Learn what you are good at and find a way to leverage your gift to create wealth. Creating a business may not be an interest of yours, but did you know you can still be an owner of a multibillion dollar company? That's right! You may not have a unique business idea of your own, time to create a business plan, or the cash to start up your own business; however, you can capitalize from other entrepreneurs. By purchasing shares of a company's stock, you become part owner of that company.

When the company does well, you make money too. The more shares you purchase from the company the more money you will make. However, as part owner, if the company growth decreases you can lose money. In fact, you can purchase stock from several other companies and be part owner of as many organizations that you can afford. Stock is a great way to create passive income and create wealth. The stock game requires courage and the ability to take risks.

The price of stocks can fluctuate over time. Several variables can affect the price. The company's CEO, reputation, marketing, economy, domestic- and international affairs, lawsuits, and competition can all influence the price. Before buying or selling stock, it is good to do some research on the company. There are many strategies you can use to help you make a decision. For starters, consult with a financial planner to help. Over time, you will develop your own research strategies to help you make decisions. Don't get discouraged and don't be afraid to fail. Remember that practice makes perfect.

"The price of stocks can fluctuate over time."

Did you know that when you put your money in a checking or saving account the bank pays you interest? You're paid interest because the bank uses your money to loan to their customers. The bank charges customers large fees for borrowing money and shares a tiny percentage of the profit with you. Someone once said, "Interest isn't interesting unless you are receiving it."

TWO TYPES OF INTEREST

The bank pays us interest because they use our money to make money. Wait, I know what you're thinking. I thought the same thing too: when we put our money in the bank it was stored in a safe place with our name on it until we needed it back--not exactly. When we deposit money into our accounts it doesn't just sit there. The money is loaned out to other customers and the bank charges the borrower large fees. The fees charged to the borrower create large profits for the banking institution. In return the bank pays us back a tiny percentage for using our money.

There are 2 types of interest the bank pays: *simple* and *compound interest.*

Simple Interest vs. Compound Interest

The bank pays **Simple Interest** only on the money that
you have deposited into your account. Here is how it
works:

CALCULATING SIMPLE INTEREST
I=prt

*EXAMPLE: You deposit $1000 in the bank and they pay
you 10% interest per year and you keep your money in
the bank for 5 years.*

I=prt

I = interest	I = ??
P = investment	p = 1000
r = interest rate	r = 10% or 0.10
t = time (years)	t = 5

I = (1000)(0.10)(5)= $500

*After 5 years of **simple interest** you will have earned
$500*

Compound Interest is different from simple interest
because you don't only earn interest on the money you
saved, but also on the interest you've earned! This is
how it works:

If you invest $1,000 (your principal) and it earns 10
percent (interest rate or earnings) per year. The first
year, you would have $1,100 your original principal,
plus 10 percent or $100. The second year, you would
have $1,210.00. This is because the next interest
payment equals 10 percent of $1,100 or $110.00.

Here is how it works...

CALULATING COMPOUND INTEREST:

Year	Principal	Interest	Principal at End
1	$1,000.00	($1000 x 10%=) $100.00	$1,100.00
2	$1,100.00	($1,100 x 10%=) $110.00	$1,210.00
3	$1,210.00	($1,200 x 10%=) $121.00	$1,331.00
4	$1,331.00	($1,331 x 10%=) $133.10	$1,464.10
5	$1,464.10	($1,464 x10%=) $146.41	$1,610.51
6	$1,610.51		

*After 5 years of **compound interest** you would've earned **$610.51***

So, which do you prefer? **SIMPLE** ☐ or **COMPOUND** ☐

Real estate, business, and stocks are the three main assets that lead to wealth. If you don't get a handle on all three, you will have a difficult time getting and maintaining wealth. Haven't you heard of people who earned millions from the lottery and lost it overnight? I believe the reason they lost it all is because they didn't understand assets vs. liabilities. I would bet that they didn't have a plan to make smart investments in real-estate, business, and the stock market.

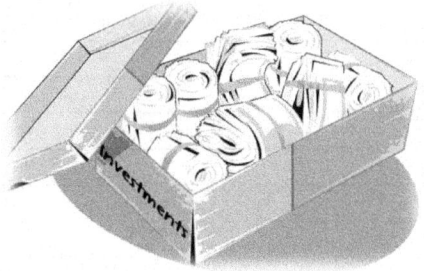

Notes

Box 4:
Keep your Game Tight
(Education)

*Rule: You can use this box toward anything that will
help you grow personally or professionally, such
as college, workshops, books, health and fitness
clubs, self defense, etc.*

The next box is dedicated to giving you an
advantage over competition. Label this box
"education." My brother used to say this quote to me
often, "A wise man knows he knows nothing and a fool
believes he knows everything." What this means to me
is regardless of how many books you may have read, or
the number of awards, certifications, or degrees you
may have received, there is always room for more
knowledge. My spiritual mentors taught me that God's
knowledge is infinite and so is the human mind;
therefore, you can never learn enough. The minute we
stop seeking knowledge is when we stop growing. The
world is constantly evolving with new ideas, new
gadgets, and new technology. There is a demand for us
to be quicker and faster. What is trendy today may be
out-of-style next month.

Technology and social media have connected the global community into one giant community. The Internet gives us unlimited access to people and information. Learning how to repair your car or build a new deck can be found online. Clothing designs, health, and financial strategies can be learned now from your home computer or smart phone. How to build business plans and resumes are a couple of the many lessons that can be learned with a click of a button. Subjects that took students years to learn at a college or university can now be achieved within a few hours. Saying you didn't know is an unacceptable excuse today. If you want information, all you have to do is get online and go get it. It's free! My brother taught me to be humble and have a thirst for knowledge. To keep up with this changing world, you must improve yourself spiritually, mentally, morally, physically, and economically. The minute you stop improving is the minute you become stagnant, which will inflict spiritual, mental, and physical death upon yourself.

At times, school may seem boring and I understand that feeling. The primary purpose for education is to help you discover who you are. The first and most important education you should receive is knowledge of self. Education should help you to learn more about yourself, all while helping to see your personal value. My spiritual mentor taught me that I shouldn't learn about chemistry. I *am* chemistry. I shouldn't learn about mathematics, I *am* mathematics. I shouldn't learn about history or economics, I *am* history and economics. Understanding your connection to these subjects helps to bring self-awareness about who

> *If you want information, all you have to do is get up and go get it.*

you are and your value to the world. When you receive a proper education and know who you are, self-confidence is developed. The greater we learn the greater the confidence. A lack of education develops the opposite—low confidence.

After you learn how to keep your game tight, it's important to understand what to do with that knowledge. We already learned that the purpose for knowledge is to learn about self and our value as it relates to the universe. What we learned is also consistent with the first law of nature, which is self-preservation.

The first assignment of every living organism is survival. Each day, everything in creation performs duties to survive. Plant life follows a system called photosynthesis. Animals graze in the field. Birds and insects spread seeds and lay eggs. Human beings harvest crops or drive to and from work. Every living thing does its part to survive. When everyone and everything does its own part, the entire life cycle is at peace.

> **When everyone and everything does its own part, the entire life cycle is at peace.**

I like to compare this peace to a beautiful sounding choir. To create harmony, each member sings a different note. The duty of each singer is to perfect their notes without being distracted by the other notes they hear. When each individual singer is gathered together to sing they create perfect harmony. The same can be applied to an orchestra, a football team, basketball team, corporation, family, community, state, or nation. The system fails when each piece in the game doesn't know its purpose and when you don't know your purpose; this throws the peace and harmony off course. Therefore, the responsibility of all living things is to get to know thyself and find one's purpose. Then use that knowledge to preserve self, family, community, and ultimately, the entire world! The more you learn, life won't be such a chore when you wake up each morning. The more you learn the more knowledge you will have to help yourself and others.

Knowledge is an asset. We should be found investing our energy, time, talent, and money to get knowledge. Make no mistake: Education doesn't only involve school. Education is anything that will help you to cultivate yourself in reflecting the power and majesty of God. Education can involve learning a new language, completing a degree or certification, buying a book, attending a seminar, joining a gym, or learning self-defense. There is so much to learn and it is your responsibility to get all that you can.

> *Education is anything that will help you to cultivate yourself in reflecting the power and majesty of God.*

Notes

Box 5:
You Get Out What You Put In (Donations)

Rule: *Use this box for contributions toward a worthy cause, such as your church, non-profit organization, school, or community center.*

The best feeling in the world is being in a position to help others. Label this box "donations." The only way you can help others is by supporting yourself first, but it doesn't stop there. You must understand that you are only one link in the chain. You must take responsibility to make your link strong by acquiring knowledge, wealth, and resources. If you fail to do so, you become a weak link and can cause the other parts of the link to overcompensate for your shortcomings. All of us get weak, but the other links must be willing to lend a hand from time-to-time. As time progresses, the support we receive from the other links build strength and gets us back in the position of helping the entire chain again. Helping one another is necessary. It is critical that we understand how we are an extension of everyone and everything around us. Everything we say and do produces an effect on something or someone. Knowing that we're a part of a bigger body than ourselves, it is our duty and responsibility to contribute as much as we can to help.

Giving is an asset. As we learned in earlier chapters, wealthy people gather more assets than liabilities. Giving produces tangible returns and supernatural returns on your investments. Some returns are not always monetary. Helping a family member, friend, or stranger can create lasting relationships worth more than diamonds or gold. Giving doesn't always include money. The situation you are trying to aid may require your time, strength, talent, or intellect. There are many ways to serve and give back. There may be an opportunity to pick up trash alongside the road. Visit the sick and shut-in to keep them company. Serve on a non-profit organization board. Feed the homeless. Donate clothes, toys, and blankets. Get involved with random acts of kindness. Be generous to someone asking for loose change, become a mentor to a child. Become a coach for a little league team. Start a neighborhood watch or clean-up community. Finally, donate money to your place of worship, school, and non-profit organizations.

"Donate money to your place of worship, school, and non-profit organizations..."

Never look down or turn your back on those who need help. We never know when it may be our turn to receive assistance or a helping hand. It is also important to give cheerfully and freely with a pure heart. In addition, don't expect a return from whoever you've helped. When you give charity, it will be paid back to you in various ways. God blesses the giver with friends from all walks of life, wealth, good homes, health, and peace of mind. The giver's reputation within their family

> *It is important to give cheerfully and freely with a pure heart.*

and community is adored. The life of a giver is prosperous and that prosperity is passed on for generations.

In addition, to receiving a reward from God for giving charity, wealthy people understand that when they give tangible gifts (i.e. money, clothes, time, toys and food), they can add up the amount and write the items off as an expense on their annual income tax statements. By keeping track of your annual giving, it decreases the amount of taxes a person will have to pay annually.

All the features and benefits previously mentioned are difficult to experience if you are living paycheck-to-paycheck. The key to having a fulfilling life is through acquiring money and resources. Without the two, you become a financial

> *Wealth and financial freedom can be achieved by us all if we set up a plan and work that plan.*

burden and weight on others. Wealth doesn't fall from the clouds. Wealth isn't achieved by winning the lottery or gambling. Wealth and financial freedom can be achieved by us all if we set up a plan and work that plan. Learn from the mistake of others, use this system for yourself, and make sure to pass it on!

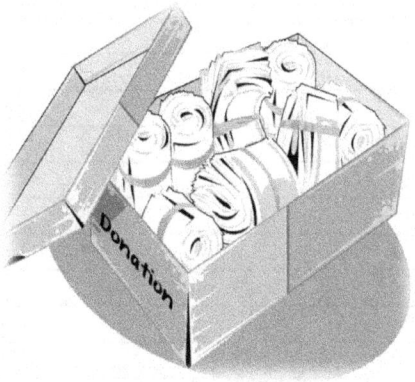

Notes

Box 6:
PLAY DOUGH
(Entertainment)

Rule: Use this box for your personal enjoyment.

I decided to save the best for last. Label this box "entertainment." By now, we should've learned that our money has more than one purpose. We learned that those who live paycheck-to-paycheck believe spending is the only purpose for money. On the flip side, the wealthy and those who are financially free understand that their income is used for multiple purposes which are for living expenses, saving, investing, education, and donations. All of these are essential in order to create financial freedom. But there's an important box we must also allocate money too. We must put aside Play Dough. If we work hard, we must play hard!

> *You owe it to yourself to enjoy what you worked hard to gain.*

You owe it to yourself to enjoy what you worked hard to gain. Life would be miserable to wake up early, commute to work, sit in traffic, work over 40 hours a week, get paid, and not enjoy what you worked hard to earn.

From your monthly income 10% should be set aside for your entertainment. Anything that brings you pleasure you should go splurge and treat yourself to a good time.

CAUTION: This Play Dough box is important but it is also the most over used. Many will rob Peter to pay Paul. Meaning: break the rules and misuse money from their other accounts/boxes to have a good time or spend money on liabilities i.e. clothes, shoes, jewelry, eating out etc. The rule is after you have spent your 10% on having a good time don't get tempted to dip in your other boxes. Each box has its purpose and must be used only for that purpose. Financial freedom is a choice and it requires delayed gratification and discipline.

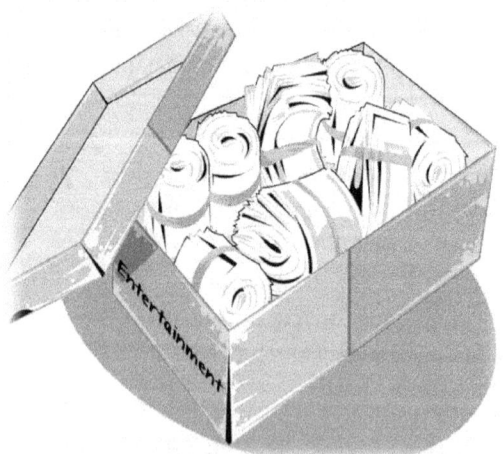

Notes

Pay Yourself First

Before you pay anyone, you come first! If you don't practice this principle, you will lose control over your finances and become a slave to your bills. This means, your income will not be used to achieve financial freedom. Instead you will be forced to work each day and use your income to pay bills. The only guaranteed method of having the amount you plan to set aside at the end of each month is paying yourself first. Don't get it twisted, paying yourself first doesn't mean that you keep all your money and have a shopping spree. Think about the trouble a business owner would have by taking all the profits and forgetting to set aside money for inventory, new equipment, payroll, and funds for emergencies. You are a business too and the same way a business must divide profits into several departments, you must do the same for yourself.

When you receive your income "pay yourself first" by taking money out for your priority boxes: *saving, investing, and education*. Attempting to pay your bills first and save the leftovers is a dangerous slippery slope. Many have tried paying themselves last and failed. The money they planned to save and invest after paying bills in most cases is never there.

Being careless and not allocating the appropriate amount of money to yourself and the other boxes is a major violation in the Money Game. Coming up next I will review the rules for the game, and discuss how much of your income will go in each box every month.

Money Management System

"The Rules to the Game"

Let's review rules to the money game. So far, you have learned that your money should be divided into different categories. Let's review those six categories and the rules again:

Boxes & Rules

➢ **Living Expenses:** "Skills to Pay the Bills" – Use money for monthly household needs.

➢ **Saving: "Don't Get Caught Slipping"** –Use this money for large purchases over $100 or emergencies.

➢ **Investments:** "Scared Money, Don't Make Money" –Use money only when it's going to make more money.

➢ **Education:** "Keep Your Game Tight" - Use money towards anything that will help you grow personally or professionally.

➢ **Donations:** "Get out what you put in" – Contributions towards a worthy cause.

➢ **Play Dough: "Entertainment"** – Use money for your personal entertainment.

Now we need to know how much of our monthly income should go into the 6 different boxes. To avoid living paycheck-to-paycheck, you must understand that your monthly income has more purpose than spending. At minimum, your monthly income should be allocated into six different places that we have already classified: Living Expenses, Savings, Investments, Education, Donations, and, Entertainment.

The following list will illustrate the amount of money you should allocate to each category.

Allocation for $1000 Monthly Income

➤ Living Expenses: "Skill the Pay the Bills"

(55% of your monthly income = $550)

➤ Savings: "Don't Get Caught Slip'n"

(10% of your monthly income = $100)

➤ Investments: "Scared Money, Don't Make Money"

(10% of your monthly income = $100)

➤ Education: "Keep Your Game Tight"

(5% of your monthly income = $50)

➤ Donations: "Get out what you put in"

(10% of your monthly income = $100)

➤ Play Dough: "Play Hard"

(10% of your monthly income = $100)

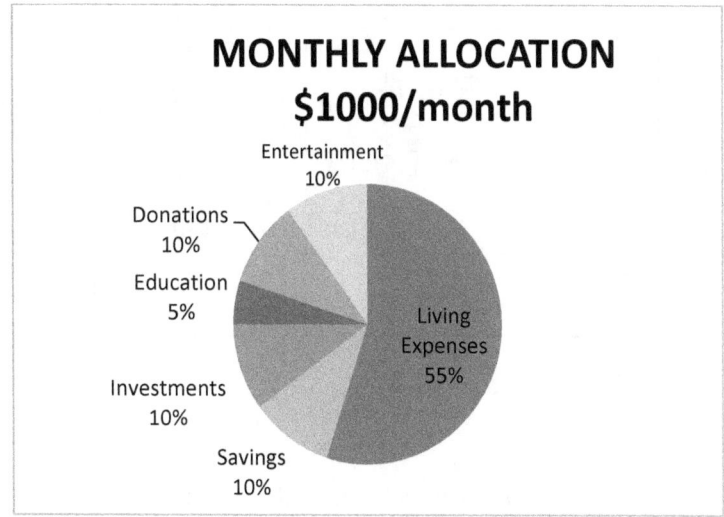

EXAMPLE - 6 MONTH FINANCIAL BUDGET

	LIV	SAV	INV	EDU	DON	ENT
Month1	$550	$100	$100	$50	$100	$100
Month 2	$550	$100	$100	$50	$100	$100
Month 3	$550	$100	$100	$50	$100	$100
Month 4	$550	$100	$100	$50	$100	$100
Month 5	$550	$100	$100	$50	$100	$100
Month 6	$550	$100	$100	$50	$100	$100
Total	$3300	$600	$600	$300	$600	$600

Add up the columns and fill-in the amounts

- ➤ Living Expenses: _____
- ➤ Savings: _____
- ➤ Investing: _____
- ➤ Education: _____
- ➤ Donations: _____
- ➤ Entertainment: _____

How much money was saved after 6 months?

_____

Now complete your own budget!

<u>Budget, Saving, & Investing Plan</u>

Monthly Income $_____

- ➤ Living Expenses: "Skills to Pay the Pay the Bills"

  (55% = $_____)

- ➤ Savings: "Don't Get Caught Slip'n"

  (10% = $_____)

- ➤ Investments: "Scared Money, Don't Make Money"

  (10% = $_____)

- ➤ Education: "Keep Your Game Tight"

  (5% = $_____)

- ➤ Donations: "Get out what you put in"

  (10% = $_____)

- ➤ Play Dough: "Play Hard"

  (10% = $_____)

6-MONTH FINANCIAL BUDGET

	LIV	SAV	INV	EDU	DON	ENT
Month1	$	$	$	$	$	$
Month 2	$	$	$	$	$	$
Month 3	$	$	$	$	$	$
Month 4	$	$	$	$	$	$
Month 5	$	$	$	$	$	$
Month 6	$	$	$	$	$	$
Total	$	$	$	$	$	$

Sum up the totals and complete the fields.

➢ Living Expenses: _____
➢ Savings: _____
➢ Investing: _____
➢ Education: _____
➢ Donations: _____
➢ Entertainment: _____

How much money will you have saved all together after 6 months?

_____

Now that you have learned the rules for money and the multiple purposes your money should be used for, I am confident that you have the foundation to win the Money Game! To win the game you must have discipline, and strategy. Once you get these rules mastered you need to make them a habit. If you follow this strategic plan, you will avoid living paycheck to paycheck and earn street credit. After mastering these concepts, be sure to pass it on to the members of your family and community.

Notes

Notes

Notes

Notes

About the Author

Khalil Abdul Aziz, Founder/CEO of Street Credit, Inc., born and raised against odds has broken society's expectation of who he should be. A native of Lansing, MI, his roots go deep where only a hustler's mentality survives. As a preteen, a business-minded man was born. From selling candy to hustling herb (and all those things in between), Aziz began developing street credit. He is an example of how we all have the power to change. He eventually found passion in sports, becoming a top-rated high school football quarterback. He is a model for youth going on the wrong path. This brother has changed his destiny.

He gives major love, respect, and recognition to his late brother Bico (his first mentor). They were the dynamic duo that created buzz around the Lansing area through their management company called Moor'Rockn Productions. Aziz later developed interest in promoting parties, recording, and marketing. Hence, the birth of Flava Entertainment, a marketing company, was born. He acquired skills in management promotion and advertisement for commercial ads and local concerts. At one point, Aziz also opened a retail store in the Lansing Mall.

In 2001, he lost his brother, friend, teacher, business partner to the same streets he had once depended on. Although his brother's passing was like a sharp pain in the chest, Aziz decided to keep going. He opened a teen night club in his brother's honor and called it Club Bicos. Aziz's reputation as a business man, marketing director, and club promoter started to emerge locally.

In 2006, he relocated to Atlanta, GA, and took interest in higher education and career development for adults. He decided to continue his education and earned a master's in business administration. And yet another level of his life unfolds, as he launched Street Credit, Inc. in 2010 to teach young people financial literacy.

Khalil Abdul Aziz is working toward Street Credit's national/global success. Aziz brings to Street Credit the structured expertise of a former club owner, savvy intellectual style of a professional promoter, and salesman's strategy that teaches you to invest in self. Over the years, his business and life experiences have led him to give back. Street Credit is the vessel he uses to reach others.

Street Credit is the major highway that connects side streets and alley ways to knowledge, love for self, and financial excellence.

Street Cred Glossary

asset - something that makes or creates money

beef up (slang) - to increase

block, or hood - neighborhood; where someone lives; a community

bread (slang) – money

break yourself off (slang) - to give to oneself

clientele - loyal customers

credit - see credit score

credit score - a number generated to measure your creditworthiness

debt - unpaid liabilities

debt slavery - to be held captive financially against one's will

financial freedom - when one has enough passive/residual income that will sustain chosen lifestyle

financial swagger - see street credit

global/international player - someone who does business globally

goal - a target that one attempts to achieve

hustle - a method of earning money

liability - something that takes money away

mentor - a coach who helps develop a person's professional growth money management - a process or system used to create financial freedom or a paycheck-to-paycheck lifestyle

opponents- individuals in opposition; someone who goes against

pay yourself first, or PYF - one gives payment to self before paying others

paycheck to paycheck (already included within text) - when a check is spent before it is received

play dough – money used for enjoyment or entertainment

profit - the amount of income that exceeds expenses

rate of interest - a number or percentage used to pay a debt

residual income - income generated from an asset

self love - to hold oneself in high regard

slippery slope - not the recommended route; dangerous; caution

slipping, or slip'n - to be caught off guard

stash - an informal savings account, usually contained in a shoebox or mattress

streams of income - multiple businesses that are generating residual income

street credit, or street credibility - when one is financially free strengths - characteristics, or skill sets, that are used to reach maximum potential

swagger - a person who has a confident posture and conducts themselves in a smooth manner

the game - trade, commerce, business

the money game - involves investments, saving, taking risks, entrepreneurship

tight (slang) - something that is good or done correctly; well put together

weaknesses - underdeveloped characteristics

wealth - to be free from debt

Answer Key

Get Ready to Start the Game

Page 50

Needs	Need or Want?
Groceries	Need
Movies	Want
Eating out	Want
Mortgage/Rent	Need
Shoes, clothes	Want
Energy Bill	Need
Credit Card Bill	Need
Daycare	Need
Candy bar	Want
The Club	Want
Video Game	Want

Page 78
Ending balance $1771.56

Page 98
How much money saved all together after 6 months?
Saving $600+ Investing $600+ Education $300 =$1500

References

Direct, I. (Ed.). (n.d.). Types of Interest. Retrieved from http://www.ingdirect.com.au/savings/tips-hints-guides/types-of-interest.html

History of McDonald's Restaurants :: AboutMcDonalds.com. (n.d.). Retrieved from http://www.aboutmcdonalds.com/mcd/our_company/mcdonalds_history_timeline.html

Johnson, A. (2013, June 24). 76% of Americans are living paycheck-to-paycheck. Retrieved from http://money.cnn.com/2013/06/24/pf/emergency-savings/

Kiyosaki, R., & Lechter, S. (1999). The cashflow quadrant: Rich dad's guide to financial freedom. Paradise Valley, Ariz.: TechPress.

Quast, L. (2013, April 15). How To Conduct A Personal SWOT Analysis. Retrieved from http://www.forbes.com/sites/lisaquast/2013/04/15/how-to-conduct-a-personal-s-w-o-t-analysis/

www.ingramcontent.com/pod-product-compliance
Lightning Source LLC
Chambersburg PA
CBHW051330170526
45166CB00002B/746